FOREWORD

Remembrance plays an important part in our country's history and this book will help children and families to learn about who we remember, and why we remember them.

When we study Remembrance, we can better understand the service and sacrifice of millions of men and women from Britain and across the world who helped to secure a better world which we enjoy to this day. Every community and family has a story to tell about those who fought for us, and hopefully this book will encourage you to learn about yours.

M Bashall

Lt General James Bashall CB CBE,
National President, Royal British Legion

The story of Remembrance begins more than 100 years ago with the First World War. The First World War was one of the most brutal conflicts in history. It lasted four years, from August 1914 to November 1918, and involved more than 30 countries.

A year after the war ended, people stopped their lives for two minutes' silence to remember those who had died or fought in the war. Many of the traditions of Remembrance began on that day, 11 November 1919.

The First World War was fought between Germany, the Austro-Hungarian Empire, the Ottoman Empire (Turkey) and Bulgaria, known as the Central Powers, and the Allies, who were Great Britain, France, Italy, Russia and the USA. Many Commonwealth countries, including pre-partition India, Canada, Australia, South Africa and New Zealand, fought the war on the side of the Allies.

Battles took place in the air, at sea and on land in France, Luxembourg and Belgium, which became known as the Western Front. There was also fighting in Russia, called the Eastern Front, and in Italy, the Balkans, the Middle East, Africa and elsewhere.

Many of the battles on the Western Front were fought from trenches dug into the ground. Men on both sides lived in these and used them as a base to launch attacks. The trenches were cold and uncomfortable, continually dirty and muddy, and full of disease-spreading rats and lice.

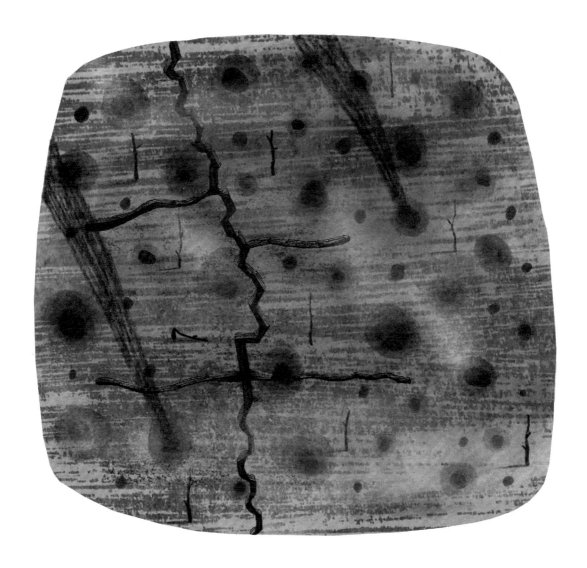

Lines of German trenches faced Allied trenches.
The land in the middle was called 'No Man's
Land'. Men crossed 'No Man's Land' to try
to capture the other side's trenches. This was
called 'going over the top'. In the attacks,
many men were hurt or killed by bullets,
artillery shells and poison gas.

10

"It was mud, mud, everywhere: mud in
the trenches, mud in front of the trenches,
behind the trenches ... I was tired of all the
sacrifice that we had there just to gain
about twenty-five yards ... "

John Palmer, British gunner

As the war continued, more people were encouraged, or forced, to sign up to fight. Whole villages of untrained men signed up, believing that it would be over soon.

Advances in technology, such as the development of machine guns, tanks and aeroplanes, meant that this war was more deadly than any previous conflict.

Soldiers fought in horrendous conditions. By the time the war ended, more than 5 million British soldiers and 3 million Commonwealth soldiers had fought. Approximately 20 million people had been killed.

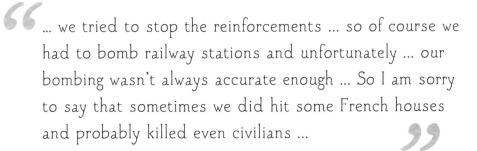

" ... we tried to stop the reinforcements ... so of course we had to bomb railway stations and unfortunately ... our bombing wasn't always accurate enough ... So I am sorry to say that sometimes we did hit some French houses and probably killed even civilians ... "

Pierre Cheret, pilot in the French Air Force

13

On 11 November 1918, after more than four years of battle and bloodshed, the fighting stopped. The Allies and Germany signed a document, called an armistice, agreeing a ceasefire. The armistice was agreed in a railway carriage in the French countryside. This day would be known in future as Armistice Day.

The war officially ended at 11 am on the 11th day of the 11th month.

People around the world celebrated. They hoped there would
never be another war like this again.

Many people never saw their family members again. Their bodies were buried in countries far away, where they had bravely fought and died.

When a soldier was killed during the First World War, they were buried in hastily dug graves close to where they died. When they could, survivors put up a wooden cross marked with the name of the dead man.

Gradually, after the war, wooden grave markers were
replaced by headstones in newly opened war cemeteries.
Gardeners created beautiful spaces here so that those who
could afford to visit would have somewhere peaceful
to remember their loved ones.

After the war, there were thousands of soldiers with no known grave. Their families had nowhere they could go to grieve. Instead people built stone war memorials that listed the names of the dead. People could come here to remember their loved ones.

Menin Gate Memorial

In Ypres, Belgium, in 1927, the Menin Gate Memorial was built. It lists more than 54,000 men who are thought to have lost their lives there.

In Turkey, the Australian government built a memorial on the site of the fiercest fighting in 1915 where thousands of lives were lost on both sides. The Lone Pine Memorial commemorates more than 4,900 Australian and New Zealand servicemen who died trying to capture the Gallipoli Peninsula and who have no known grave.

Lone Pine Memorial

The Canadian National Vimy Memorial stands on Vimy Ridge in France. It was built to remember the 60,000 Canadians who died during the war.

Canadian National Vimy Memorial

On 11 November 1919, the first Armistice Day was held. Named after the Armistice agreement, the day was a way to honour those who had lost their lives in the war. A service of Remembrance was held in churches. People prayed for peace and hoped for a better future.

From then on, it was decided that every 11 November would be a day of Remembrance.

"The first stroke of eleven produced a magical effect. The tram cars glided into stillness, motors ceased to cough and fume, and stopped dead ... Everyone stood very still ... The hush deepened. It had spread over the whole city ..."

Manchester Evening Guardian, 12 November, 1919

In 1915 the Canadian soldier and poet Lieutenant Colonel John McCrae
wrote the poem 'In Flanders Fields' about the war and the poppies
he'd seen growing on the battlefields. Poppies were the first flowers
to grow on the battlefields after the fighting had ended. Their red colour
is a symbol of the blood shed and their growth is a sign of new life.

In Flanders fields the poppies blow
Between the crosses, row on row,
That mark our place; and in the sky
The larks, still bravely singing, fly
Scarce heard amid the guns below.

From 'In Flanders Fields'

American Moina Belle Michael was so affected by the emotion of this poem that, after the war ended, she campaigned for the poppy to become a symbol of Remembrance across the United States. The idea soon spread to other countries.

Inspired by Moina Belle Michael, Anna Guérin, from France, decided to make poppies and sell them to raise money for ex-servicemen and women.

Today this tradition continues, and in many countries people donate money and wear a paper poppy at Remembrance time. The money raised goes towards helping soldiers and their families.

Different-coloured poppies have been made by charities
and organisations. Purple poppies are to remind us
of all the animals, such as horses and dogs, who
also lost their lives during war.

In the 1930s, some people started to wear white poppies to promote peace. They hoped a war would happen never again.

" ... I wear a white poppy alongside my red one, because I know they fought and so many died for my peace, our peace. "

Michael Morpurgo, author

Nearly twenty years after the first Remembrance service, in September 1939, Germany invaded Poland and the Second World War began. Germany's leader, Adolf Hitler, wanted Germany to be a powerful country again. He wanted to control more land in Europe.

This war was longer and more deadly than the First World War.
Sixty countries and hundreds of millions of people were involved.

At first, the battles in the Second World War were fought in Europe.
Germany invaded Poland in 1939, then France and Belgium in 1940.
Later, the fighting spread to Russia, Africa and Asia and beyond.
In 1941, Japan attacked US battleships at Pearl Harbor, Hawaii.
After this, the USA joined the war on the Allied side.

Aerial bombing raids happened across Europe and were terrifying for those living in towns and cities. Both sides dropped bombs, often during the night. The bombs killed many people and destroyed houses and buildings.

" ... it's the most terrifying experience to stand there, hearing these bombs from a distance and them getting louder and louder and louder, wondering how many have they got left and are you going to be the next one? "

Alan Hartley, Air Raid Precaution messenger

When the war ended in 1945, 40–50 million people had been killed
and millions more had been injured. Over 6.5 million men and
women joined the armed forces from Britain, and over 6 million
from Commonwealth countries.

It was the biggest and most destructive war in history.
Huge parts of the world had been reduced to ruins.

33

In Great Britain, most communities hold their commemorations on Remembrance Sunday, which is the nearest Sunday to November 11th. That way, more people can attend because it isn't a working day.

During Remembrance people remember in many different ways – as individuals and as part of their community.

At some Remembrance services, just as they have done for the past hundred years, a bugler will play the *Last Post*. This was a call that told military service men and women that it was the end of the day. It is sometimes played at military funeral services and symbolises that the duty of the dead is over and they can now rest in peace.

"
Went the day well?
We died and never knew.
But, well or ill,
Freedom, we died for you.
"

by John Maxwell Edmonds

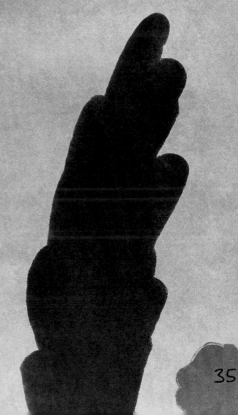

At 11 am on Armistice Day, a two-minute silence is held during which people can think about those who have died or been injured during conflicts.

After the silence, sometimes a bugler plays the 'Reveille' or 'The Rouse', a call used to tell members of the military that it's time to wake up. It symbolises that life goes on.

After the two-minutes' silence, members of the local community lay their wreaths at the bottom of war memorials. They are often poppy wreaths, but other flowers with a special meaning for different communities are also used.

At the Cenotaph in London, members of the Royal Family lay poppy wreaths on Remembrance Sunday. War veterans young and old march past the memorial as a sign of respect.

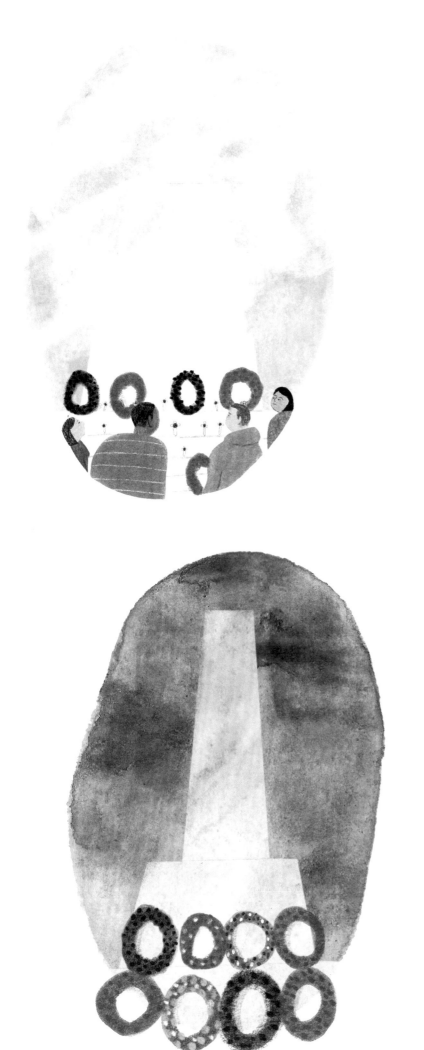

Wreaths have been used since ancient times to celebrate bravery and as a sign of respect. Their shape represents the circle of life.

Remembrance happens in many countries
around the world. In the United States, it is
called Veterans Day. It was given this name
in 1954, at the end of the Korean War,
to honour all war veterans.

In Australia and New Zealand, people come together to remember on Anzac Day, which is 25 April. On this day in 1915, Anzac soldiers began a long, hard and fierce battle at Gallipoli in Turkey. Many men died there.

Remembrance is a time for us to stop and think
about the sacrifices men and women around the world
have made for their countries.

It is a time to remember all the people who have been injured or lost their lives in conflicts around the world, from the First World War to the present day.

"When you go home, tell them of us and say for your tomorrow, we gave our today."

John Maxwell Edmonds, quoted on the Kohima War Memorial, India

'In Flanders Fields' by John McCrae

In Flanders' fields the poppies blow
Between the crosses, row on row,
That mark our place; and in the sky
The larks, still bravely singing, fly
Scarce heard amid the guns below.

We are the dead. Short days ago
We lived, felt dawn, saw sunset glow,
Loved and were loved, and now we lie
In Flanders fields.

Take up our quarrel with the foe;
To you from failing hands we throw
The torch; be yours to hold it high,
If ye break faith with us who die
We shall not sleep, though poppies grow
In Flanders Fields.

'We shall keep the faith' by Moina Belle Michael

Oh! you who sleep in Flanders Fields,
Sleep sweet - to rise anew!
We caught the torch you threw
And holding high, we keep the Faith
With All who died.

We cherish, too, the poppy red
That grows on fields where valor led;
It seems to signal to the skies
That blood of heroes never dies,
But lends a lustre to the red
Of the flower that blooms above the dead
In Flanders Fields.

And now the Torch and Poppy Red
We wear in honor of our dead.
Fear not that ye have died for naught;
We'll teach the lesson that ye wrought
In Flanders Fields.

'For the Fallen' by Laurence Binyon

With proud thanksgiving, a mother for her children,
England mourns for her dead across the sea.
Flesh of her flesh they were, spirit of her spirit,
Fallen in the cause of the free.

Solemn the drums thrill: Death august and royal
Sings sorrow up into immortal spheres.
There is music in the midst of desolation
And a glory that shines upon our tears.

They went with songs to the battle, they were young,
Straight of limb, true of eye, steady and aglow.
They were staunch to the end against odds uncounted,
They fell with their faces to the foe.

They shall grow not old, as we that are left grow old:
Age shall not weary them, nor the years condemn.
At the going down of the sun and in the morning
We will remember them.

They mingle not with their laughing comrades again;
They sit no more at familiar tables of home;
They have no lot in our labour of the day-time;
They sleep beyond England's foam.

But where our desires are and our hopes profound,
Felt as a well-spring that is hidden from sight,
To the innermost heart of their own land they are known
As the stars are known to the Night;

As the stars that shall be bright when we are dust,
Moving in marches upon the heavenly plain,
As the stars that are starry in the time of our darkness,
To the end, to the end, they remain.

Glossary

aerial in the air

air raid an attack in which bombs are dropped from aircraft

Air Raid Precaution messenger people who helped to keep people safe during air raids

Allies the group of countries that fought against Germany in the Second World War

Anzac a soldier in the Australian and New Zealand Army Corps

artillery shells a container that is filled with explosives and fired from large guns

bugle a musical instrument

bugler someone who plays a bugle

campaign actions taken, such as writing letters or making speeches, to raise awareness of your goals and make a change

carnage the killing of a large amount of people during war

ceasefire to stop fighting

cemetery a place where dead people are buried

Central Powers the countries of Germany, the Austro-Hungarian Empire, the Ottoman Empire (Turkey) and Bulgaria who fought together in the First World War

civilian a person who is not serving in the armed forces or the police

commemorate to honour the memory of, or to show respect for, someone or something

conflict a fight, battle or war

grieve to feel great sadness

gunner a soldier, sailor or airman who fires a large gun or cannon

machine gun an automatic gun that fires bullets one right after the other as long as its trigger is pressed

poison gas toxic gases that can kill

reinforcements sending more soldiers to help

sacrifice to give up something to help others

symbolise an object that represents something else

tanks a large vehicle used in war

territory an area of land that belongs to a country

tradition a belief or custom that is handed down from adults to children over many years

tragedy a very sad event that has caused great suffering and destruction

tram cars a type of transport

Further information

Books

Only Remembered edited by Michael Morpurgo (Corgi, 2016)
Poppy Field by Michael Morpurgo (Scholastic, 2018)
Private Peaceful by Michael Morpurgo (Harper Collins, 2016)
Remembering the Fallen of the First World War by Sarah Ridley (Franklin Watts, 2019)
Remembrance Day (*Great Events* series) by Gillian Clements (Franklin Watts, 2016)
Remembrance Day (Why Do We Remember? series) by Izzi Howell (Franklin Watts, 2018)
The First World War/The Second World War (*Fact Cat* series) by Izzi Howell
  (Wayland, 2020)
The Story of the First World War for Children by John Malam (Carlton, 2018)
Where the Poppies Now Grow by Hilary Robinson and Martin Impey (Strauss House
  Productions, 2014)

Websites

www.britishlegion.org.uk/get-involved/remembrance/about-remembrance/the-poppy
Find out more about why the poppy is a symbol of Remembrance

www.britishlegion.org.uk/get-involved/remembrance/teaching-remembrance
Useful resources for teachers

www.bbc.co.uk/bitesize/topics/zqhyb9q
Information about the First World War

www.iwm.org.uk/learning/resources/remembrance-in-the-first-world-war
Find out more about Remembrance on the Imperial War Museum website

www.natgeokids.com/uk/discover/history/general-history/first-world-war/
Facts about the First World War

Index